ORCA
Think

Question, connect and take action to become better citizens
with a brighter future. Now that's smart thinking!

LET'S GET CREATIVE

ART FOR A
HEALTHY PLANET

Jessica Rose

illustrated by Jarett Sitter

ORCA BOOK PUBLISHERS

Published in Canada and the United States in 2024 by Orca Book Publishers.
orcabook.com

Library and Archives Canada Cataloguing in Publication
Title: Let's get creative : art for a healthy planet / Jessica Rose ; illustrated by Jarett Sitter.
Names: Rose, Jessica (Author of Let's get creative) | Sitter, Jarett, illustrator.
Series: Orca think ; 14.
Description: Series statement: Orca think ; 14 | Includes bibliographical references and index.
Identifiers: Canadiana (print) 20230485162 | Canadiana (ebook) 20230485170 |
ISBN 9781459832145 (hardcover) | ISBN 9781459832152 (PDF) | ISBN 9781459832169 (EPUB)
Subjects: LCSH: Art—Environmental aspects—Juvenile literature. | LCSH: Art and society—Juvenile literature. |
LCSH: Climatic changes—Social aspects—Juvenile literature. | LCSH: Sustainability—Social aspects—Juvenile literature.
Classification: LCC N8217.E28 R67 2024 | DDC j704.9/4933372—dc23

Library of Congress Control Number: 2023942422

Summary: Part of the nonfiction Orca Think series for middle-grade readers, this illustrated book examines how
artists are using their creativity to help the environment and build a more sustainable world. Includes examples of
eco-art from around the globe.

Orca Book Publishers is committed to reducing the consumption of nonrenewable resources in the
production of our books. We make every effort to use materials that support a sustainable future.

Orca Book Publishers gratefully acknowledges the support for its publishing programs provided by
the following agencies: the Government of Canada, the Canada Council for the Arts and the Province
of British Columbia through the BC Arts Council and the Book Publishing Tax Credit.

Cover and interior artwork by Jarett Sitter
Design by Dahlia Yuen
Edited by Kirstie Hudson

Printed and bound in South Korea.

27 26 25 24 • 1 2 3 4

For Jordan, Ellis and Iris—my small team of adventurers who challenge me to look at the world purposefully and sustainably every day.

CONTENTS

INTRODUCTION

THERE'S NO QUESTION THAT CREATING ART makes our lives better. Just think about how happy you feel when you're dancing, singing, painting or crafting. But have you ever stopped to think about how creating art makes the *world* better too?

Artists in North America and across the globe are putting the environment first, using their ***creativity*** to build a more ***sustainable*** world. Their work isn't just beautiful to look at. Some artists are helping protect animal habitats, reclaim damaged natural environments, aid ***biodiversity*** and restore ecosystems. In this book you'll read about artists who work *with* the environment rather than disrupting it. They use natural materials and sustainable practices that don't damage Earth's resources. They use discarded and salvaged materials like plastic straws or water bottles. Even entire industries—like building design and fashion—are taking significant steps to reduce their impact on the planet.

This sculpture of a bald eagle was created using plastic and other debris that washed ashore. If you look closely, you'll see a toothbrush!

LU A PRESCOTT/SHUTTERSTOCK.COM

You'll also be introduced to thought-provoking artists who are inspiring people of all ages to care for and respect the environment. They're using their work to raise awareness about local and global environmental crises, including climate change, air and water pollution, and habitat loss. They're sparking important conversations and positive social action. They're building and engaging communities, and activating change in human behavior and public policy.

This book defines art as any creative work that a person makes to express themself. It focuses mostly on visual art, although you're probably already familiar with other artists who share their feelings through music, poetry, dance or other art forms. Many of the artists you'll meet on these pages are professional artists. This means that making art is their job. But remember, you don't have to be a professional artist to make art that makes the world a better place.

BEYOND THE CANVAS

Whether you're designing a bee habitat for **urban** pollinators or crafting a sign using sustainable materials to raise awareness about the climate crisis, the art you make matters. One of my favorite things to do, whether I'm at home or traveling somewhere I've never been before, is to visit art galleries and museums. When I was younger, I thought the best art in the world was found in places like the Louvre in Paris, the Museum of Modern Art (MoMA) in New York City or the National Gallery of Canada in Ottawa. Sometimes that's true. However, art that hangs on a gallery wall is just one type of art.

The best thing about art is that it's *everywhere*. It's in the clothing you wear, the design of buildings around you, the video games you play and the products you use. Making art

Pollinator houses are interesting sculptures, but they're not just for looking at. These structures provide bees and other pollinators with a place to nest. A pollinator's house uses materials that simulate a pollinator's natural nesting habitat.

BEEKEEPX/GETTY IMAGES

can mean building, planting or fixing something with your hands, as long as you're using creativity!

While some art you read about in this book might be found in a gallery, much of it is public art. Public art is, quite simply, art that is found in shared community spaces. It can take many forms, including murals, sculptures, landscape design and performance. My favorite art is found in places you'd least expect to find it. I love walking through my neighborhood and spotting a mural I've never seen before or glancing up at an innovative or unique building design. Whether I'm on a busy street corner or in a public park, these examples are even more powerful when I know they're having a positive impact on the natural world.

As you read this book, I hope you challenge ideas that you already have about art. Most important, as you read about artists and creative industries that are reducing their ecological footprints, think about how your own art can be purposeful. Artists are making Earth a cleaner and greener place—and having a lot of fun while doing it. The best part is, you can too!

You never know where you might find the perfect art supply. Just look at this art installation made by an artist in India using waste such as plastic bottles.

ONE
CREATIVITY FOR CHANGE

WHEN YOU THINK ABOUT ART, do you think of the *Mona Lisa* or another famous painting hanging on an art gallery's wall? If so, you're not alone! For centuries people have been asking the question "What is art?" While some might argue that certain types of art are more valuable or important than others, that's simply not the case. Art is everywhere, and it *all* matters.

More than ever, there are unique places where you can enjoy art. In this chapter you'll discover many examples of artists who are not only using sustainable art materials but are also reducing their environmental footprint by showcasing their work in parks or other outdoor spaces.

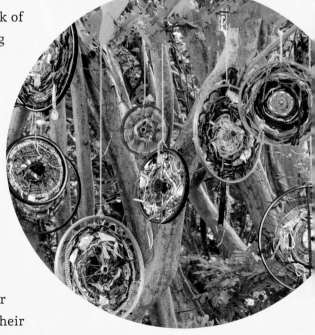

Look up! Art can be everywhere. Public art is often found in places where many people gather, like parks and streets. Bicycle rims and other trash from Florida beaches were used to create this colorful public display in Hollywood, FL.
SUNSHOWER SHOTS/SHUTTERSTOCK.COM

REDUCING THE IMPACT OF ART

A lot of conversations are happening in the art world about the impact art and art galleries have on the environment. Not all art supplies are environmentally friendly, and neither are the spaces where art is exhibited. Staging a large art exhibition can require shipping art around the world, which contributes to air or water pollution. Art galleries also use a lot of energy to operate. Let's read about some art, and artistic movements, that put sustainability first.

WHAT IS ENVIRONMENTAL ART?

That's a big question, and you might get a different answer depending on whom you talk to.

Environmental art is made sustainably by artists who are passionate about **environmentalism**. Some people call it *environmentally friendly* art or *eco-art*. Environmental art can bring art out of traditional settings. You might find it in a park, etched into a landscape or made from materials found in nature. Some art is also connected to larger art movements, such as earthwork (see "Art Works" sidebar).

Environmental art might raise awareness about an important cause. Environmental art can bring entire communities together with the shared purpose of protecting the environment. It can also explore an artist's relationship with the world around them.

ART WORKS!

Earthwork is also known as *land art* or *earth art*. It is art that is made by shaping land itself or by using natural materials, including rocks, soil, or tree branches. Sometimes earthwork is small enough to be displayed in an art gallery. Sometimes it's huge, like Robert Smithson's *Spiral Jetty* (1970), located on the shore of Great Salt Lake in Utah. It was made from 6,000 tons (6,096 metric tons) of black basalt rock and earth.

CHARLES E UIBEL/SHUTTERSTOCK.COM

We can all reduce our environmental impact when creating art. Using sustainable, recycled or reused materials encourages us to take a more responsible and conscious approach to creativity.

ALISTAIR BERG/GETTY IMAGES

This mural created by schoolchildren in Hamilton, ON, is located beside a pollinator garden that welcomes butterflies, birds, wild bees and many other types of insects.

CAROLYN ZANCHETTA

The Gallery Climate Coalition is an international community of arts organizations working to reduce the art sector's impact on the environment. The charity has a goal of cutting the sector's carbon dioxide emissions by at least 50 percent by 2030. It also promotes zero waste by encouraging galleries to reuse materials for as long as they can before replacing them.

ART IS FOR EVERYONE!

Public art is often citizen-led, meaning it's planned and created by ordinary community members—like you! Because it is found in public spaces, including parks and on the outsides of buildings, it's art that is free to view. It's sometimes found in natural spaces that encourage environmentally friendly activities like walking and cycling. Many public art projects are created with *accessibility* in mind, so that people who use wheelchairs or other mobility devices can enjoy the work.

ART IS EVERYWHERE!

Public art sometimes *revitalizes* neglected urban spaces. For example, you might find art on the side of an abandoned building or in a parking lot. In Hamilton, Ontario, the Beautiful Alleys project is making neglected alleys more inviting with colorful murals. Its vision is to clean up and beautify lanes and alleys so that people of all ages can enjoy them safely.

Some artists find locations that have been damaged by weather or natural disaster and beautify them with art. Hurricane Katrina in New Orleans left many abandoned buildings in its wake. Artists turned six of them, including a former bakery, into art installations meant to inspire people who lived in or are visiting the area.

Beautiful Alleys is a volunteer-run organization in Hamilton, ON, that promotes safe, accessible and environmentally friendly spaces for people of all ages and abilities. This mural is one of more than a dozen murals you'll find as part of the project.
JESSICA ROSE

LET'S LOOK AT ART

ᐄᓂᐤ (ÎNÎW) River Lot 11∞ Edmonton's Indigenous Art Park

📍 Edmonton, Alberta

Edmonton's first Indigenous art park is called ᐄᓂᐤ (ÎNÎW). That's a Cree word that means "I am of the Earth." The park features six works of public art by Indigenous artists. One example is *mamohkamatowin (Helping One Another)* by Jerry Whitehead, an artist from the James Smith Cree Nation in Saskatchewan. His artwork features two turtles with colorful mosaics on their backs. A mosaic is a pattern or image made by arranging individual pieces of stone, glass or another material. One unique thing about this piece of art is that it's meant to be touched and even sat on. Kids are encouraged to climb gently on the turtles' backs. This beautiful art park encourages visitors to enjoy Edmonton's landscape while thinking about their own connection to the natural world around them.

The High Line

New York City, New York

You probably know that New York City is a busy place. However, the High Line gives visitors a quiet spot in which to relax and reflect. This former railway spur now features walkable natural spaces, public art by national and international artists and art performances. Unlike your average art gallery, it's open every day of the year. And it's free! The High Line is dedicated to creating a healthy and connected community. It's also focused on the health of the planet. The project's many sustainable practices include using plants grown locally, composting all garden waste on-site and avoiding the use of harmful pesticides and chemical fertilizers.

Our Common Woods

Halifax, Nova Scotia

Located in a public park called the Halifax Common, *Our Common Woods* is a public art project featuring the work of five artists: Alan Syliboy, Erin Philp, Theo Heffler, Gary Staple and Steve Sekerak. Each artist created a sculpture using wood that otherwise would have been wasted. *Our Common Woods* is a celebration of trees and everything they do for our communities. Unlike other works of art, some of these pieces are meant to be touched and interacted with.

Art found on and around the High Line in New York City transforms the park into a vibrant outdoor gallery with sculptures, murals and other works of art that visitors can enjoy alongside nature.
MIA2YOU/SHUTTERSTOCK.COM

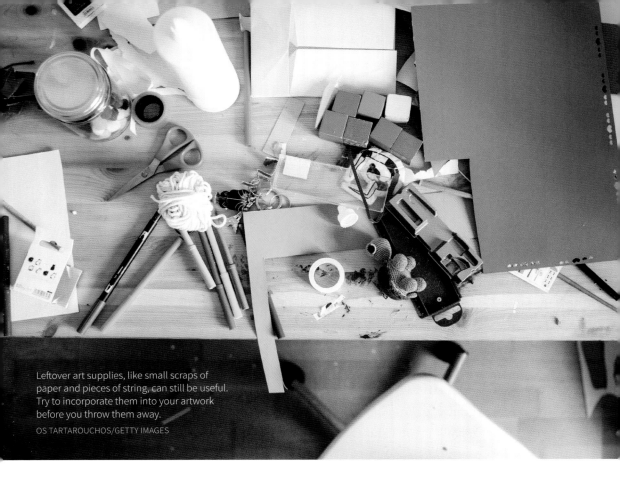

Leftover art supplies, like small scraps of paper and pieces of string, can still be useful. Try to incorporate them into your artwork before you throw them away.
OS TARTAROUCHOS/GETTY IMAGES

SUSTAINABLE ART MATERIALS

Choosing art supplies that don't damage the environment is an important part of being an eco-friendly artist. Some of the materials you use, including glitter or spray paint, might have a negative impact on the environment. Creating art can also be wasteful. For example, stickers are a fun way to decorate things, but they're usually made from plastic or foil. This means they'll remain in the environment long after you become bored with them. Try using one sticker instead of many. The good news is, there are sustainable art-making options, and they're not only for professional artists. You can buy art supplies made from recycled materials or even make supplies that don't harm the environment.

GOODBYE, GLITTER!

Who doesn't love glitter? It's flashy and can be used to decorate many things. You find it on birthday cards, in cosmetics and on clothing. You've probably used it while making art. However, glitter is usually made of tiny particles of a **polymer** called polyethylene terephthalate (PET). Those particles are **microplastics**, which are harmful to aquatic species when they get washed down the drain. And that's exactly where glitter goes when you wash it off your hands or clothing. In 2021 the *Journal of Hazardous Materials* released the first study to test the effects of glitter on the environment. It looked at both glitter manufactured using PET plastic and glitter made using alternative materials. Results showed that both types of glitter can damage aquatic ecosystems. The only difference was that the biodegradable glitter led to a notable increase in New Zealand mud snails, an **invasive species**.

Using eco-friendly glitter can reduce your environmental impact while still allowing you to be creative. This cupcake was decorated with edible glitter made from sugar.

JENNIFER A SMITH/GETTY IMAGES

PESKY PLASTICS

Aquatic species, including zooplankton, may mistake sparkly glitter for food. This can introduce dangerous chemicals or metals into the food chain. Microplastics are known to harm the fertility, growth and survival of marine life. They can end up on our own plates if they're ingested by seafood we eat.

Glitter accounts for a small amount of the microplastics found in the world's oceans, lakes and rivers. According to the *New York Times*, it makes up less than 1 percent of the microplastics that pollute the environment. But that doesn't mean glitter is harmless. Most scientists agree that any reduction of microplastics is a positive step forward.

If you're looking for an alternative, make your own edible glitter! Gorgeous glitter that tastes good too? Yes, please! You make it with granulated sugar, food coloring and a little bit of elbow grease.

ART WORKS!

In 2019 the Richmond Arts Centre in Richmond, British Columbia, made a big announcement. It banned glitter! This news made headlines across the country, but Todd Evanger, an arts programmer at the center, says the glitter ban is just one example of how the center is continually evaluating its practices and studio materials. The center is also focusing on:

- Eliminating the use of googly eyes, plastic straws and other single-use plastics
- Recycling and reusing clay and other materials
- Foraging for clay (that means collecting from the natural environment)
- Upcycling materials to be used in art programs

PAINT POLLUTION

Chances are the paint you're using is safe, especially if you're using water-based paint. Some paint, however, such as oil paint, includes toxic materials that are harmful to people and the planet. Colorful dyes, especially those used in clothing, also pollute air, water and soil—but more on the fashion industry later!

WHAT CAN YOU DO?

Making your own paint and dye for art projects is a creative way to experiment with colors. In fact, as long as people have been making art, they've been making their own paint and dye. This fun project will also help reduce food waste if you use food scraps you'd otherwise throw away.

Here are just a few natural items you can use to make paint or dye:

Until the 1850s, almost all dyes were made from natural sources—vegetables, plants and even insects. For example, red fabrics found inside King Tut's tomb are believed to have been dyed with madder root pigment. Today chemicals are used to give fabric its vibrant colors. Water is polluted when clothing factories dump these chemicals into wastewater.

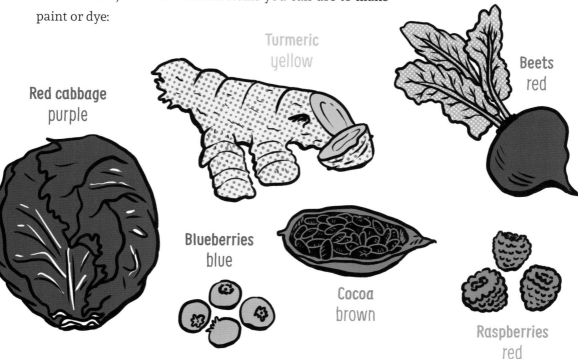

Turmeric
yellow

Beets
red

Red cabbage
purple

Blueberries
blue

Cocoa
brown

Raspberries
red

Meet an Artist Who Puts Sustainability First: *LESLIE LEONG*

📍 Whitehorse, Yukon

More than ever, artists are thinking about the impact their work has on the world around them. Meet Leslie Leong, a visual artist with a purpose. She uses **unorthodox** materials to express herself. She calls herself a visual artist focused on recycling and sustainability.

Leong, who lives and makes art in Whitehorse, Yukon, says she sees beauty and value in everything around her. You will often find her rummaging through recycling stations and **landfills** for materials to reuse and repurpose in her art. She also uses natural materials, including stone and **permafrost**—yes, permafrost!

"In an ecosystem, waste materials like dead leaves, trees and other organic matter decompose and make nutrients in the soil for new growth to spring up and thrive," says Leong. "The piece missing in our society is that most of our waste is not turned

back into useful materials. We send it to the landfill, where it breaks down into smaller bits and pieces."

Leong doesn't just make one type of art. She began working in photography and ceramics. Now her work includes printmaking, sculpture and jewelry. Her project *Melt* began with ethically collecting 485 pounds (220 kilograms) of permafrost from Tuktoyaktuk, Northwest Territories. Leong used permafrost that would not affect the future stability of anything on the surface, including homes and utilities. The permafrost melted in her front yard, leaving a small amount of solid matter behind. This debris was displayed beside a full-size 3D sculptural representation of the original permafrost. The project included a time-lapse video of the melting permafrost. She hopes this work raises awareness about the impact of the climate crisis on Arctic communities.

Influencing Others through Art

When Leslie Leong isn't making her own art, she's working with young people, encouraging them to be purposeful in their artmaking. She believes that a person's values can be reflected in their art. "For example, if the person is concerned about the volumes of garbage we are producing in our society, then use materials that are slated for the garbage or recycling," she says.

Leong thinks that choosing sustainable or reclaimed materials in art makes artists see waste differently. "This is training their brains to think creatively, to think outside the box and learn *ingenuity*," she says. She's used plastic milk jugs and DVDs in her art. Much of her work could be considered creative reuse (more on that in the next chapter).

"Everything I set my eyes upon could be a material for something," she says. "There is no need to buy new materials, except perhaps screws, nails, glues and other means of attaching things together. Now I can't help but see materials that I know would be great for something. I just don't know what that 'something' is at the time!"

"If I can't reduce human consumption of stuff, stop companies from producing goods to break down, or change the world, then what could I do? I can only control my actions and hope to influence others."

—Leslie Leong

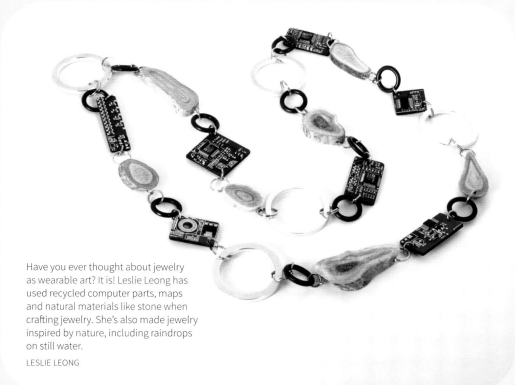

Have you ever thought about jewelry as wearable art? It is! Leslie Leong has used recycled computer parts, maps and natural materials like stone when crafting jewelry. She's also made jewelry inspired by nature, including raindrops on still water.

LESLIE LEONG

TWO
CREATIVE REUSE AND FOUND ART

YOU DON'T HAVE TO LOOK FURTHER than a garbage can or recycling bin to know the world is filled with products meant to be used once and then thrown away. Take a peek inside the trash and you'll see plastic straws, water bottles, takeout containers and junk mail. Each year the world generates nearly two billion tons (more than two billion metric tons) of waste. While some of this waste is recycled, most of it goes to landfills. Some ends up in our waterways, endangering plants and animals and polluting drinking water.

The best way to solve the world's trash problem is to reduce the amount of waste that is produced. Another helpful thing to do is reuse it. There are many ways to turn trash into treasure. We just have to think creatively!

From 2002 to 2018 the total amount of solid waste generated in Canada increased by 16 percent.

WHAT A WASTE!

Most trash that is thrown into a garbage can ends up in landfills. Some is burned, which can create air pollution, **land disturbance** or water pollution. Canada currently has more than 10,000 landfills. In 2018, 146 million tons (132 million metric tons) of municipal solid waste was sent to landfills in the United States. That's a lot of trash! Landfills might be unsightly to look at, but they cause much bigger problems too. Decomposing organic waste in landfills produces a gas that is mostly methane. Methane is a powerful greenhouse gas that traps heat in the atmosphere. It is a leading cause of the climate crisis. Landfills cause approximately 20 percent of Canada's methane emissions.

THE PROBLEM WITH PLASTIC AND PAPER

Plastic's **durability** is one reason that this **synthetic** or semi-synthetic material is used to make so many things. You'll find it in packaging, vehicles, medical equipment and even the clothes you're wearing right now. However, plastic takes about 400 years to decompose, and some estimates say it takes even longer than that if it decomposes at all. So something that is useful for just a few minutes can remain in the environment for generations! In Canada, more than one-third of plastics are created for single-use products or packaging. Canadians use almost 57 million straws every day and almost 15 billion plastic bags each year. While single-use plastics are convenient, they've created an environmental crisis. All that waste is adding up!

We can help reduce microplastics in the environment by being mindful about the art supplies we use, choosing eco-friendly alternatives.

DEEMERWHA STUDIO/GETTY IMAGES

Every year about 7.9 tons (8 million metric tons) of plastic waste enters the world's oceans. Even more can be found in other waterways, such as lakes and rivers. Plastic waste threatens marine animals, including seabirds, turtles and seals, who can be severely injured or killed when they become tangled in trash.

You've heard a lot about plastic waste, but what about paper waste? Making paper products requires huge amounts of energy and water. It also contributes to **deforestation**, which reduces biodiversity and contributes to the climate crisis. In the United States, paper accounts for 25 percent of landfill waste and 33 percent of municipal waste. The average household throws away 13,000 pieces of paper every year. Paper packaging and junk mail are leading examples of paper waste.

This aerial photograph shows trees that have been cut down in New Zealand. Recycling paper is a good option, but it's not a solution to deforestation. We must reduce the amount of paper being used in the first place.

TAHREER PHOTOGRAPHY/GETTY IMAGES

Plastic Mero is a sculpture created by Portuguese street artist Artur Bordalo, who is also known as Bordalo II. He made it using plastic waste collected from the waters around Medeira Island in Portuga

ESIK SANDOR/SHUTTERSTOCK.COM

CREATIVE REUSE

Creative reuse is the process of turning unwanted items into things you can use. Thanks to your imagination, old or discarded goods can become something completely different. Creative reuse reduces trash, **diverting** it from the **waste stream**, in fun and innovative ways!

Creative reuse is also called upcycling or repurposing. And it's something we can *all* do.

LET'S LOOK AT ART

Some artists raise awareness about waste and other environmental concerns through memorable, innovative works of art. One might build a towering sculpture, assembling hundreds or even thousands of individual pieces of trash.

Another might have a subtler approach, creating jewelry or pottery out of scrap materials that would otherwise be discarded. Let's look at a few examples of creative reuse.

The Heidelberg Project
🌐 Tyree Guyton, United States

Located in Detroit, the Heidelberg Project is an outdoor art environment that aims to improve people's lives through art. It began in the 1980s when painter and sculptor Tyree Guyton visited Heidelberg Street, where he grew up. He was sad to see that the street had been neglected and people in the neighborhood were struggling with poverty, addiction and violence. Along with his grandfather, he began cleaning up the neighborhood. They transformed vacant lots and abandoned houses into art sculptures. He used discarded materials considered waste to represent the neglect he saw on the street. Since the 1980s, the project has continued to grow. The Heidelberg Project is now an arts organization that uses art to spark conversations about important topics, including poverty and race.

iThemba Tower
🌐 Johannesburg, South Africa

You'll find the iThemba Tower in the garden of the Spaza Art Gallery in Troyeville, Johannesburg. It's a looming figure assembled from unlikely materials—7,000 plastic bottles purchased from local waste collectors. The installation, created by r1., a Johannesburg-based contemporary street artist, decorates a 66-foot (20-meter)-high cellular tower that is no longer used. The iThemba Tower lights up at night, illuminating the importance of recycling. r1.'s public art pieces aim to create visual conversations with local residents. His other projects have revitalized spaces by using such reclaimed or recycled materials as wood pallets and CDs.

Gaia

📍 Edmonton, Canada

A study released in 2022 by the World Health Organization found that more than 85,600 tons (87,000 metric tons) of health-care waste was generated during the COVID-19 pandemic. Students at Lillian Osborne High School in Edmonton had a creative solution. They created Gaia, a company that turns single-use masks into something sustainable and fashionable—jewelry! Masks are collected, sanitized, melted, cut and then crafted into necklaces and earrings. Students hope the project inspires global action toward a cleaner planet for future generations.

In 2021 McDonald's Canada announced that it would use paper straws instead of plastic straws, as well as replace other single-use plastics. To celebrate this achievement, McDonald's partnered with a company in Kelowna, BC, and 15 Canadian and Indigenous artists for a unique art project. Each artist produced an original piece, using a tray made from upcycled McDonald's plastic straws as a canvas.

FOUND ART

Another example of creative reuse is found art. Artists use random junk they find in everyday life—from household appliances to scrap metal or wood—to create works of art. The objects used are completely ordinary, but they can be crafted into something extraordinary!

Found objects have been used to create art for centuries. In the 20th century, a number of famous artists incorporated unexpected objects into their art. In 1915 Marcel Duchamp, a French American painter and sculptor, started using the term *readymade* to describe some of his art. He took everyday objects, often those that were mass-produced, and changed them from their original purpose into art. Duchamp used such items as a bicycle wheel, a snow shovel and even a urinal in his work. Spanish artist Pablo Picasso also used found objects in his art. In a 1942 piece, he used a bicycle seat and handlebars to create a bull's head.

Found art encourages us all to look at everyday objects differently. It also challenges the idea of what is considered **fine art**. Before Duchamp's *Bicycle Wheel* (1913), nobody would have considered a bicycle wheel mounted on a wooden stool to be art! Today it's considered one of Duchamp's most important pieces.

These whale sculptures displayed on Patong Beach in Phuket, Thailand, were made from marine litter, including flip-flops, children's toys and waste from food and drinks.
FPSKILLER/SHUTTERSTOCK.COM

This recycling center in Durham, NC, is a place where artists can find art materials that otherwise might have been discarded. Creative reuse centers turn discarded materials into treasures by encouraging artists to rethink and repurpose them.

ART WORKS!

You're most likely to find a creative reuse center in a larger city. If there isn't one close by, don't fret! You can hold your own art-supply swap. Ask your teacher if you can organize an exchange in your classroom, or plan one with friends. Encourage each friend who is participating in your swap to bring three to five items to exchange. Maybe they have magazines or colorful paper scraps they're no longer using. They could also collect natural items like pine cones or shells. A swap is a great way to take home new-to-you supplies to craft with!

SKIP THE STORE

If you're running low on art supplies, you might head to a craft or **big-box store**. If you live near a creative reuse center, however, there may be another option. These centers collect and distribute unwanted, **surplus** or discarded materials that can be bought or taken for free by people in a community and reused. These usable materials are diverted from landfills and give creative people a place to find inexpensive (or free), high-quality materials. The centers also give artists a chance to try out new skills and experiment with unfamiliar supplies with little risk.

Creative reuse centers are organizations run by volunteers with a passion for art and sustainability. They provide art materials to other charitable organizations, including those that serve kids who might not have the money to purchase expensive art supplies. These important creative hubs also give manufacturers and businesses a place to donate unwanted or unneeded materials that otherwise would end up in the trash. They're also great gathering places for artists to share ideas and build community.

Here are a few examples of creative-reuse centers in North America:

Regina's Art Supply Exchange is an organization in Saskatchewan that offers affordable secondhand art materials for artists and art educators of all ages and practices.

ArtsJunktion mb Inc. is a community-based charitable organization in Winnipeg. It is committed to redistributing reusable materials using a take-what-you-need, pay-what-you-can model. ArtsJunktion also has a tool-lending library. Members of the library are able to borrow dozens of arts, crafts and hand tools to use at home, work or in their studios.

Creative Reuse Toronto is a not-for-profit organization that reuses wasted resources as a tool to teach people about art, creativity and the environment. During the COVID-19 pandemic, Creative Reuse Toronto focused on reclaiming materials from businesses and industries that were closing or downsizing.

Materials for the Arts in New York City collects surplus materials and redistributes them free of charge to schools and not-for-profit organizations focused on making art.

SUPPLY Victoria is British Columbia's first creative reuse center. The organization is an inclusive community hub that offers affordable and sustainable art supplies. The space is also used to host events and workshops that teach people how to upcycle waste into art.

The Green Project in New Orleans, Louisiana, has a salvage store that diverts two million pounds (907,185 kilograms) of waste from landfills every year. The Green Project also collects and recycles usable latex and water-based paint, mixing it into new colors. This innovative paint-recycling program prevents an incredible 40,000 gallons (181,844 liters) of paint from being improperly disposed of and potentially damaging local ecosystems.

The ReUse Depot at the Ontario College of Art and Design University in Toronto is a collection of spaces where usable art and design materials can be left for other art makers. Student artists and designers who attend the university can take material to upcycle and repurpose. This helps reduce the financial barriers some students face when purchasing art supplies.

Equitable Access to Art

Everyone has a right to make art! However, some art supplies—including canvases, oil paints and sculpting materials—are expensive to purchase. Creative reuse makes art supplies accessible to *everyone* at a low cost.

THE CIRCULAR ECONOMY

Did you know that waste is a human creation? In nature it simply doesn't exist. Ecosystems are circular. This means that nothing is wasted. For example, when a plant or animal dies, it decomposes with the help of nature's recyclers. Nature's recyclers include snails, slugs, worms and **microbes** that help break down organic matter.

When you're making art from materials you've gathered at an art-supply swap, you're participating in the *circular economy*. It's a system that keeps products and materials in use. Instead of things being thrown away, they are reused, repaired, repurposed or recycled. The circular economy is different from the more-traditional linear economy. In a linear economy, *raw materials* are made into a product that is eventually discarded. The circular economy extends the life of products and helps eliminate waste.

In a circular economy, manufacturers design products that are reusable or last for a long time. Products are also designed to be repaired more easily. Unfortunately, that's not the norm right now. Just think of a cell phone. It's estimated that the average person replaces their cell phone every two years or less.

"By taking waste materials and remaking them into beautiful, functional new objects, I demonstrate by example that we too can create a circular economy, " said artist Leslie Leong (whom you met in the last chapter). She uses her art to raise awareness about electronic waste—also known as e-waste. She's even incorporated computer circuit boards into her work.

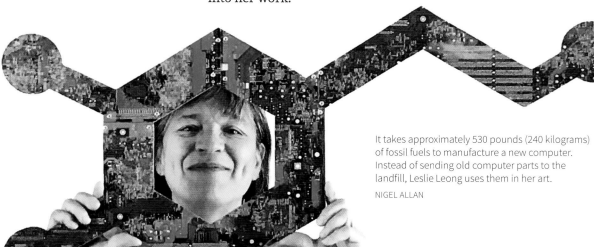

It takes approximately 530 pounds (240 kilograms) of fossil fuels to manufacture a new computer. Instead of sending old computer parts to the landfill, Leslie Leong uses them in her art.
NIGEL ALLAN

THE REPAIR ECONOMY

When something breaks or becomes damaged, your instinct might be to toss it in the trash. Whether it's your bike, a favorite pair of jeans or a beloved toy, there's another option— repair it! Repairing something isn't always possible, especially if you don't know the ins and outs of fixing electronics. But many times there's a simple solution that people just don't think about. Repairing something can be *a lot* of fun! The repair economy allows people just like you the chance to work with their hands, be creative and learn new skills, all while extending the life of a product. One way you can participate in the repair economy is to attend (or plan!) a repair café. It's a gathering where citizens fix things and learn from one another. These cafés are held in cities all over the world!

Green Venture is an environmental education organization in Hamilton, ON. Its repair cafés encourage participants to fix broken household items, including small electronics, furniture and clothes.

GREEN VENTURE REPAIR CAFE

Repairing something is an excellent way to prolong the life of an item while also allowing you to work with your hands. With the help from some tools and a new coat of paint, your skateboard might look as good as new!

ROMA BARELKO/SHUTTERSTOCK.COM

Meet a Member of the Repair Economy: JASON ALLEN

📍 Hamilton, Ontario

When Jason Allen was a kid, he loved building and fixing things, taking them apart to see how they worked. As he got older, he convinced himself he wasn't good with his hands. He compared himself with his dad, who was good at *everything*, and with his brother, a sculptor and wood carver.

Eventually Allen realized he didn't have to be an expert at anything. He could be creative by making functional, practical things. When he discovered **leatherwork**, his friends started asking him to fix things like slippers and belts.

Allen decided to turn his hobby into something that would help the environment. He committed to a year of repairing things, including clothes, shoes and home appliances, instead of replacing them. "It was hugely satisfying," says Allen. "It kept a ton of things out of landfills, and saved me a lot of money (close to a thousand dollars)!"

Allen was invited to his first repair café. He volunteered to fix leather goods and do basic furniture repair. "In every case, the person I did the repairs for was so grateful for my repairs and so happy they could keep using the item. Not a single person was upset that the item didn't look brand new!" he says.

Since then Allen has continued repairing items and attending repair cafés. He says that a huge part of participating in the repair economy is getting over the idea that you need to buy the latest, trendiest things to impress people. "It's also a radical, revolutionary act in a society that judges your worth by how much stuff you own." Allen has many ideas about how young people can participate in the repair economy. Here are a few of them:

Think about the life cycle of a product before you buy it. When you buy something, think about what will happen to it once you no longer need it. Can your new computer or cell phone be repaired, or will you throw it away? Take a moment to think about whether you *really* need it at all.

Avoid shopping for fun. Purchase what you need and buy the best quality you can, even if it means saving up for something instead of buying the cheapest version. Many inexpensive things are designed not to be repairable.

Don't be afraid to be creative! Try to repair something like a favorite sweater or a piece of furniture yourself. You'll be surprised what you can do with a needle and thread, some superglue, duct tape or a few well-placed screws. Even if things don't work out, likely you'll have learned a new skill or at least had fun while trying.

JEFF TESSIER

"A huge part of participating in the repair economy is to get over the idea of buying things to impress people. If that's your goal, you'll always be looking to upgrade to the newest, fanciest version of things. Repairing means you're stretching the life of a product far longer that it is meant to be stretched."

—Jason Allen

WHAT CAN YOU DO?

Inspired by the art and artists you've read about in this chapter? There are many ways you can create your own zero-waste (or almost waste-free) art. All you have to do is use items that otherwise might have been thrown away or recycled.

Start by looking around your own home. To inspire you, here are just a few items that can be upcycled into works of art:

Have you ever thought about how many pumpkins go to waste every Halloween? Next year make a jack-o'-lantern from a tin can. You can use it over and over again!

LEO FERNANDES/SHUTTERSTOCK.COM

Egg cartons	Old greeting cards	Cardboard boxes
Newspapers	Gift wrap	Elastics
Fabric scraps	Magazines	Buttons
String or ribbon	Paper scraps	Plastic or glass bottles or jars
Bottle caps	Empty toilet-paper or paper-towel rolls	

Here are a few art projects to get you started:

Build a terrarium in a mason jar.

Create a banner using scraps of paper and string.

Craft a "guitar" using a shoebox, empty paper-towel roll and some elastics for strings.

Make a lantern by punching holes in a tin can. (Put a candle inside to light it up!)

Create a wind chime using discarded metal objects, including tin-can lids, cutlery and keys.

Make a scarf or headband from a sweater or T-shirt that is beyond repair.

A terrarium is an easy gift you can make using recycled and natural materials.
WESTEND61/GETTY IMAGES

IMPORTANT TIPS!

Be sure to ask a parent or guardian for permission before you start salvaging household items. It's important to check that they're actually waste before using them. If you're rescuing items from the recycling bin, such as plastic bottles or tin cans, make sure they're thoroughly cleaned and there are no sharp edges before you use them.

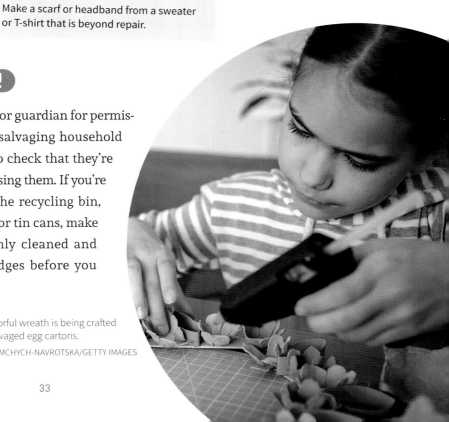

This colorful wreath is being crafted from salvaged egg cartons.
MARIA SYMCHYCH-NAVROTSKA/GETTY IMAGES

THREE
SCIENCE,
ART AND DESIGN
COME TOGETHER

ART HAS ALWAYS BEEN INSPIRED by the landscapes and biodiversity of the natural world. But have you ever thought about how the natural world benefits from art? You've already read about art that sparks conversation about important environmental issues and how art can be made sustainably. Art can also offer solutions to some big environmental problems, including habitat loss and the effects of climate change. Art and science can come together in truly innovative ways!

HELPING HABITATS

Earth's species, both on land and in water, are losing their homes at an alarming rate. Various human activities have led to environmental crises, such as climate change, deforestation and **habitat fragmentation**. According to a report from the Intergovernmental Science-Policy Platform on Biodiversity

Filter: Tower is a sculpture by the TH&B Collective (Simon Frank, Dave Hind, Ivan Jurakic and Tor Lukasik-Foss) that examines the intersection of rural, urban and industrial environments. You'll often see birds like this one visiting the artwork in Hamilton, ON.

JESSICA ROSE

and Ecosystem Services (IPBES), human actions have significantly changed three-quarters of the land-based environment and about 66 percent of the marine environment. The good news is that clever arts-based solutions are ensuring that some species still have a place to live.

ARTIFICIAL CORAL REEFS

Among one of the oldest ecosystems on our planet, coral reefs have inhabited the world's oceans for more than 200 million years. Known for their biological diversity, they're home to more than a quarter of all ocean-dwelling creatures.

Coral reefs grow very slowly and are extremely fragile. They're vulnerable to many threats, including climate change, physical damage or destruction from coastal development, and harmful fishing and boating practices. Pollution from urban stormwater runoff, untreated sewage and land-based activities like forestry and agriculture can block sunlight. This consumes oxygen that coral reefs need for *respiration*. Garbage found in waterways can get tangled on reef organisms, which also blocks the sunlight needed for *photosynthesis*.

Marine conservationists and artists might have different areas of expertise, but when they work together, they can help restore coral reefs. Artificial coral reefs are underwater structures that mimic the look of a natural coral reef. Made of natural or synthetic material, they provide a stable area for *coral polyps* to attach, encouraging regrowth. The reefs also act as excellent habitats for many species of fish. And they're art!

UNDERWATER SCULPTURES

Jason deCaires Taylor is a sculptor who is committed to helping coral reefs thrive. He builds his installations on land, and they're transported by crane to their permanent homes on the ocean floor. Taylor says he places his works of art "down current from natural reefs so that after spawning, there are areas for them to settle." He does this using low carbon, pH neutral materials that allow coral polyps to easily attach.

While just one of Taylor's underwater sculptures would have attracted *some* wildlife, the British sculptor had bigger plans. He's created a number of underwater gardens that feature many sculptures in one place. The first was Molinere Bay Underwater Sculpture Park, located off the west coast of Grenada in the Caribbean Sea. The garden features an incredible 75 works of art that cover an area of 8,611 square feet (800 square meters)! The sculptures are located between natural rock formations. They can be seen by scuba diving, by snorkeling or from a glass-bottomed boat.

Underwater art? Why not! Visitors to the Museum of Underwater Art can experience art while scuba diving or on board a glass-bottom boat.
ROB ATHERTON/SHUTTERSTOCK.COM

Shipwrecks and other human-made objects on the ocean floor can act as synthetic coral reefs. According to the National Centers for Coastal Ocean Science, rocky reefs, artificial reefs and shipwrecks are ecologically valuable habitats for a wide range of marine species, from reef fishes to top predators.

JEFFREY HAMILTON/UNSPLASH.COM

Students in Burlington, ON, worked with the Hamilton Conservation Authority to create nest and habitat boxes for local wildlife. They used their carpentry skills to build bat habitats, turtle-nest protectors and tree-swallow boxes.

TAKING SHELTER!

Carolyn Henne, a professor at Florida State University, created *Sea Stars,* a 10,000-square-foot (929-square-meter) sculpture made of a one-of-a-kind biodegradable material called Oyster Catcher. If you were looking at it from above, you'd see life-size sculptures of synchronized swimmers alongside a 50-foot (15-meter) octopus. *Sea Stars* was installed on a sandbar, with the goal of attracting oyster larvae. What makes it unique is that sometimes you can hardly see it at all. When the tide is high, the artwork is submerged. That's when oyster larvae have the chance to attach. The oyster reef will also provide shelter for fish, crabs and birds.

ART WORKS!

Artistic partners Mary O'Brien and Daniel McCormick create sculptures they say "have a part in influencing the ecological balance of compromised environments." (*Compromised* means "vulnerable" or "weakened.") Their work has benefitted wildlife, watersheds and forests. One habitat installation, called *Foraging Island*, was built on a former city dump in Palo Alto, California. The wooden sculpture has helped rebuild a habitat for a number of species, including burrowing owls and hawks. People of all ages and abilities were invited to help build the installation. Sixty-five local volunteers worked for nearly 200 hours. *Foraging Island* looks like a stretched-out bird's nest. It was made using branches, sticks and other trimmings from Palo Alto trees that otherwise would have gone to waste.

River Fork Ranch Flood Plain (2014) by Mary O'Brien and Daniel McCormick was created with the help of hundreds of volunteers who harvested willow branches. The sculpture anchors soil, prevents erosion and provides animal habitats.

©WATERSHED SCULPTURE. PHOTOGRAPHER: MARY O'BRIEN

3D-PRINTED HABITATS

3D printing is the process of creating three-dimensional solid objects by layering materials (usually plastic) according to instructions in a computer. The process is already being used in innovative ways in the medical community. Archireef, a Hong Kong company with expertise in marine biology and 3D printing, is using the technology to rebuild ecosystems. It printed and installed 128 pieces of terracotta tile at Hoi Ha Wan Marine Park. The tiles mimic the shape of a type of coral called *platygyra*—also known as worm brain or brain maze coral. The tiles are an example of **biomimicry**.

Archireef Academy, which offers ocean literacy programs, hosts workshops for kids, youth and adults. In this photo, a young participant is using a 3D pen to create a colorful reef tile.
ARCHIREEF

UN-BEE-LIEVABLE ART!

You've probably heard that bees are in trouble. That's because pesticides, disease, air pollution and loss of habitat are leading to their decline. Bees are pollinators that are essential to help grow the food we eat. We wouldn't have many fruits, vegetables and even chocolate without their hard work. Did you know that there are over 20,000 species of bees around the world? There are more than 850 species in Canada alone! Scientists are scrambling to find solutions to the pollinator problem. But you don't need to be a biologist or an ecologist to be a bee ambassador. Artists are helping to save the bees too!

This apiary sculpture, designed by Evan Hutchinson, was installed at Bridgeport Industrial Park in Richmond, BC. It's an example of public art with a purpose, providing a home to pollinators.

MELANIE DEVOY, COURTESY OF THE RICHMOND ART GALLERY

GEOFF CAMPBELL, COURTESY OF THE RICHMOND ART GALLERY

Meet an Artist Passionate about Pollinators: CAMERON CARTIERE

📍 Vancouver, British Columbia

Cameron Cartiere is an artist, researcher and professor at Emily Carr University of Art + Design in Vancouver, British Columbia. She's working with other artists and community members of all ages to create art that aims to bring bees back to urban areas. Border Free Bees is a series of public-art projects that aim to raise awareness about the problems pollinators face and empower communities to work together to create solutions for habitat loss—through art. Border Free Bees transforms underused spaces into pollinator pastures with wildflowers that benefit bees, butterflies and birds.

One example of a Border Free Bees project is the Bridgeport Public Art Pollinator Pasture. Located at the Bridgeport Industrial Park in Richmond, BC, it's a living earthwork. It features wildflowers that benefit pollinators, planted in pleasing ways. For example, some were planted in the shape of giant bumblebee wings—sort of like a mural that could be seen by people in planes flying overhead.

Students at a nearby secondary school participated in the project by planting 600 sunflowers. They cared for the seedlings and produced a sunflower wall that was inviting to pollinators. Eco-artist Sharon Kallis participated too. She worked with community members to harvest Himalayan blackberry vines, which are an invasive species. The vines were used to create beautiful sculptures shaped like butterfly nets.

The Terra Nova Public Art Pollinator Meadow, also in Richmond, is another Border Free Bees project. Artist Jaymie Johnson worked with students at Terra Nova Nature School to create "bumble baskets" made from plant material found nearby. These tiny sculptures act as sanctuaries for bees that visit the garden. Some of Border Free Bees' pollinator pastures include apiary sculptures, which are functional works of art with design elements that provide shelter to bees.

A Safe Place to Land

It's clear that Cameron Cartiere is passionate about bees! But bees aren't the only pollinators she's hoping to protect through art. She wanted to improve the public's relationship to birds as well. Her project *As the Crow Flies* was a six-month-long public-art event that took place along a 6.2-mile (10-kilometer) route that went through several Vancouver neighborhoods, making it one of the longest public art installations in Canada.

As the Crow Flies included three separate art projects, including one called *Nesting Nests*. It contained hundreds of nests for birds native to Vancouver, from tiny hummingbirds to huge eagles. Individual nests made by community members were put together to create one giant bird nest. Another project was *Fledglings*, designed by Cartiere and ceramic artist and educator Jess Portfleet. The installation featured 6,000 ceramic baby crows made by people in community centers across Vancouver. Cartiere and Portfleet spent six months teaching members of the public how to use molds to make the tiny sculptures. Each represented one of some 6,000 crows that fly across Vancouver daily.

"The whole process of making these birds was really about community engagement," says Cartiere, adding that people of all ages participated in the project. The birds were displayed all together as a celebration of our feathered friends while also raising awareness about the dangers they face living in a city. Then members of the public were encouraged to take a bird sculpture home.

Six thousand ceramic baby crows were created over several months at community workshops as part of the *As the Crow Flies* installation, an example of collaborative art.

COURTESY OF CAMERON CARTIERE

"My garden is my most beautiful masterpiece"

—Claude Monet

USE YOUR GREEN THUMB FOR GOOD!

Gardening, like many other creative hobbies, is proven to have a positive impact on mental health. It can lower stress and boost self-esteem, and is an enjoyable way to connect with nature. Gardens can also be spectacular works of art, incorporating design principles like structure and balance. A well-designed garden can also benefit pollinators.

A rain garden has an important job to do. It collects stormwater runoff, including rain and snow, preventing it from entering storm drains and waterways. This is important because stormwater that comes in contact with streets and lawns can carry pollutants, including fertilizers, pesticides, pet waste, road salt and trash. Rain gardens help reduce flooding, improve soil and water quality, and reduce **erosion**. They also provide food and a place for wildlife to live.

A PARADISE FOR POLLINATORS

Artist Alexandra Daisy Ginsberg wondered if art and technology could help protect pollinators. The result was Pollinator Pathmaker, an online tool that uses *artificial intelligence (AI)*. It designs gardens by choosing and arranging plants that will benefit as many pollinator species as possible. To create the tool, Ginsberg worked with pollinator experts, horticulturalists and an AI scientist. Once a user designs a garden, they can see a digital artistic rendering of what their colorful garden will look like. Pollinator Pathmaker has been used by huge public gardens, including The Eden Project in Cornwall, England. People who want to have pollinator-friendly gardens in their own backyards also use this tool. Pollinator Pathmaker is an artwork app informed by science.

Gardening is a form of design, especially when you're planting with pollinators in mind. Intentionally selected and placed plants help provide food and habitats to urban pollinators.
TRONG NGUYEN/SHUTTERSTOCK.COM

Forgot your phone charger? Don't worry! *The Energy Tree* uses solar energy. It's beautiful to look at, but it also lets visitors charge their phones with energy harvested from the sun.

RENEWABLE ENERGY ART

By now you've probably realized that pretty much anything can be used to make art. That includes solar panels! Solar panels convert sunlight into energy that can be used to make electricity. They might seem like an unlikely art material, but some artists have found creative ways to use them.

The Energy Tree, created by designer and sculptor John Packer, is a 15-foot (4.6-meter) metal tree located in Millenium Square in Bristol, England. At the end of each metal branch is a solar panel "leaf" pointed in a specific direction. This functional sculpture harnesses the sun's energy to produce power. The sculpture provides people with Wi-Fi and places to charge their phones.

The Energy Tree is just one example of a renewable-energy sculpture. Another example is *Sun-Catcher*, a sculpture in Florida by public artist Deedee Morrison. Made in part from recycled aluminum and solar panels, it captures the sun's energy during the day. At night the sculpture glows a vibrant yellow when it is lit up by solar energy.

Shala Akintunde is a Nigerian multidisciplinary artist. He creates solar-powered murals and sculptures that showcase the beauty of solar energy. One example of his work, *Shala's Bronzeville Solar Pyramid*, is a 16-foot (5-meter) pyramid in Chicago that generates solar electricity. The pyramid is covered with symbols designed by high school students in the city. Akintunde hopes this piece and others like it will raise awareness about technologies that use **renewable energy**.

ART WORKS!

Some artists use wind to create their masterpieces. Anthony Howe is a kinetic artist who creates wind-driven sculptures. The word *kinetic* means "relating to motion." Kinetic art includes moving elements, or it requires motion for its effect—for example, viewers might be required to move around in order to fully experience the art. Howe's work can be found in many places around the world, including in Montreal. His piece *Di-Octo II* is located at Concordia University. The sculpture has pieces that look like tentacles, which open and close as wind blows.

RAINWATER SCULPTURES

In the Arte Sella Sculpture Park in Borgo Valsugana, Italy, you'll find *Reservoir*, a sculpture that collects rainwater. American artist John Grade, who created the sculpture, says he's inspired by geological and biological forms and systems in the natural world. It's made of 5,000 individual pouches that capture falling rain. As the rain gathers and eventually evaporates, each pouch, which looks like a person's open hand, changes its shape and position. The captured rainwater contributes to a humid environment that helps local vegetation and wildlife thrive.

You probably don't think of pine trees as perfect places to hang art. John Grade's installation *Reservoir* is made up of 5,000 individual pieces that are carefully supported by trees.

ED BUZIAK/ALAMY STOCK PHOTO

LET'S LOOK AT ART

You've already read about a few artists who are using their creativity to build a more sustainable world. Here are a few other projects to inspire you to think differently about how and why we make art.

Living Seawalls

📍 Sydney, Australia

The panels that make up Living Seawalls are created using 3D-printed technology similar to what you read about earlier in this chapter. Based in Sydney, Living Seawalls is a partnership between the Sydney Institute of Marine Science and Reef Design Lab, a company that works closely with scientists to help marine habitats. The panels are designed to mimic natural shoreline structures such as the roots of mangrove trees and they have tiny holes that provide homes for marine organisms that help filter out pollutants, cleaning the water.

Living Water Garden

📍 Chengdu, China

This spectacular public park is located on China's Fu and Nan Rivers. But it's not your average public park. It's also a fully functioning water-treatment plant. It features a natural wetland water-cleaning system, interactive art sculptures and an education center.

Living seawalls are proof that marine construction can be part of a solution. Through creative design, they benefit marine life while also educating people about development practices that harm waterways.

ALEX GOAD, COURTESY OF LIVING SEAWALLS

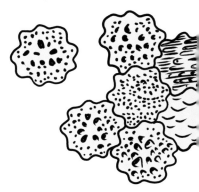

Some examples you've read about in this chapter fit the definition of *ecovention*. This term was first used in 1999 by Sue Spaid, a **curator** and art professor. She defines ecoventions as "inventive, practical actions with ecological intent."

Citizen science empowers people of all ages, including kids, to actively participate in scientific research. You can contribute valuable data that can lead to positive environmental change, all while practicing your photography skills!

WANTED: CITIZEN SCIENCE PHOTOGRAPHERS

Designing and installing a huge sculpture isn't something we can all do. But that doesn't mean you can't help scientists solve major problems, especially if you have a creative eye and a knack for photography. You can become a citizen scientist! Snapping photos of the world around you can be more than an enjoyable hobby. Your shots can help scientists who are gathering data on everything from light pollution to declining pollinator populations.

Citizen science is research done by volunteers who observe and record the world around them. A citizen scientist might help scientists monitor water and air quality, changing habitats, or the amount of litter in your neighborhood. Many projects simply require you to upload photos you take to an app or an online hub like *iNaturalist* or *SciStarter*. You can also take part in a bioblitz, an event in which volunteers find and identify as many species as possible in a specific area during a short time period.

WHAT CAN YOU DO?

Here are a few citizen-science projects you can get involved in:

Stream Selfie connects thousands of citizen scientists who collectively monitor water quality—the health and cleanliness of water. Photographers take pictures of local streams and upload them to an online database. These photos help assemble an ever-growing map of waterways across the United States and beyond. When photographers add photos to the database, they also answer questions about a stream's health. For example, did they spot any garbage? This information is used to determine which streams might be unsafe for humans.

Journey North encourages people to use technology to help conserve and protect migratory species, including hummingbirds, monarch butterflies and robins. Photographers contribute images of sightings that help scientists track migration patterns. Your photos are plotted on a map that anyone can see online.

People all over the world are already seeing their daily lives affected by the climate crisis. Citizen scientists participate in ISeeChange projects to document changes in the environment, weather and climate in their own neighborhoods. One consequence of the climate crisis is flooding. A number of ISeeChange projects ask people to take and post pictures of flooding they see. This information is synced with weather and climate data. Your photos can be used by cities as they prepare for future flooding events.

You can participate in citizen science anywhere. Biodiversity is all around you, including in your backyard, on your balcony or in a community garden. It's ready to be photographed!

FOUR
IMAGINATIVE DESIGN FOR A BETTER FUTURE

WHEN YOU SHOP ONLINE OR WALK INTO A STORE, you're presented with a *lot* of choices. Sure, it might be tough to decide if you want a blue shirt or a red one. You might prefer shoes with laces or ones that slip on. However, the choice you're making is much more important than color or style. When you purchase a product or service, you're picking which company you will support with your **purchasing power**.

PUTTING THE ENVIRONMENT FIRST

More than ever, consumers are demanding that the businesses they support care about environmental issues, including climate change and pollution. This is especially important to young people making purchasing decisions. A 2021 survey of consumer attitudes toward sustainable shopping in the United States found that Gen Z people

Corporate social responsibility is based on the idea that a business can reduce its negative impact on people and the planet. It's also about reducing harm through practices and policies that treat employees fairly and protect the environment. Corporate social responsibility might include a business's commitment to prioritizing sustainable practices or materials or encouraging employees to volunteer their time to causes they care about.

(those born between the mid-1990s and early 2010s) are more likely to buy sustainably than are older generations. The younger generation is also influencing others to change their buying behavior.

You've read about individuals making sustainable choices when creating art. But what are businesses, institutions and entire creative industries doing to benefit the environment? It turns out some of them are doing a lot! Leaders in architecture, fashion and other creative industries are putting the environment first. In doing so, they're also raising awareness about important issues like habitat fragmentation, wildlife fatalities, excessive waste and pollution.

ECO-ARCHITECTURE

Look around! Every building that surrounds you is a work of art. In fact, each is the result of hundreds of decisions made by an architect. An architect is someone who works in architecture, which is the art and science of designing buildings. Architects are responsible for the overall vision of a building's design, including its size and shape and the materials it's built from. An architect designs a functional piece of art in which people live, work or play.

Architects aren't the only people responsible for building a house, university or skyscraper. Engineers, landscape designers and entire construction teams work together to build them. Unfortunately, new structures can be bad for the environment. According to the Canada Green Building Council, buildings generate up to 30 percent of all greenhouse gases and 35 percent of landfill waste. They also consume up to 70 percent of municipal water.

Eco-architecture, also known as sustainable architecture and eco-friendly architecture, aims to reduce its impact

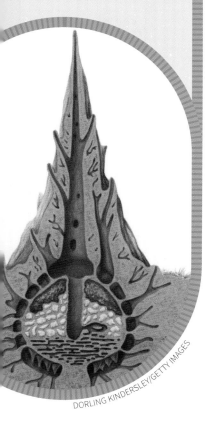

ART WORKS!

Some buildings are inspired by things in nature. The Eastgate Centre, an office and shopping complex in Harare, Zimbabwe, was inspired by, of all things, termites! Its climate-control system mimics the structure of termite mounds. Termites build their mounds with tunnels inside and air vents outside, opening and closing the vents to regulate the temperature. The design lets air flow through easily.

DORLING KINDERSLEY/GETTY IMAGES

on the environment as much as possible. This kind of architecture is an example of *ecological design*, which is about creating products and services that minimize damage to the environment and encourage sustainability.

BUILDING GREEN

So what makes a building eco-friendly? Well, a lot of things! Eco-architecture uses materials and building practices that are ethical, sustainable and nontoxic to people and wildlife. Whether a building is brand new or being renovated in new and innovative ways, there are ways to reduce its environmental impact over its entire life cycle. This can be done through the building's design, construction, maintenance and, in some cases, demolition. Building green can include minimizing a building's energy use through innovative technologies, like wind or solar power, and can also include a means of harvesting rainwater to be used elsewhere in a building. Salvaged, reclaimed or recycled building materials that are harvested or processed sustainably can be used.

These colorful panels on the Pixel Building in Melbourne aren't just eye-catching. They provide shade that helps reduce the building's energy consumption.

NORMAN ALLCHIN/SHUTTERSTOCK.COM

Some of the buildings you've read about have achieved Leadership in Energy and Environmental Design (LEED) certification. LEED status is regulated by the US Green Building Council, which aims to create buildings that are better for the environment and human health. They also have the goal of protecting and enhancing biodiversity, and reducing their contribution to the climate crisis.

Jessica Rose

LET'S LOOK AT ART

The results of eco-architecture are beautiful sculptures that provide people with safe, sustainable places in which to live and work. Let's look at a few examples.

Pixel Building
📍 Melbourne, Australia

The Pixel Building is one of the most colorful buildings in the world, but is far more impressive than that! This building, known as one of the greenest on Earth, is Australia's first *carbon-neutral* office building. Its exterior isn't only stunning to look at. Colorful panels provide shade, reducing the need for cooling. Wind turbines generate energy, and innovative toilet technology reduces water consumption. A garden on the building's roof collects and filters rainwater, which is then used throughout the building.

Centre for Sustainable Development
📍 Montreal, Quebec

The Centre for Sustainable Development provides space for citizens and industry leaders to meet and share ideas about sustainable development. It's fitting that some people consider it the greenest building in Canada. Among its many sustainable features are experimental concrete slabs made in part by powdered glass from recycled bottles, drywall made from 99 percent recycled materials, and a living wall with 400 plants that act as a natural air filter. A cistern (tank) harvests rainwater, which is redirected to the building's toilets. When it was built, an incredible 90 percent of the construction waste was diverted from landfills.

Bahrain World Trade Center

♥ Manama, Bahrain

Winning awards for its use of renewable energy, the Bahrain World Trade Center looks a little bit like a sailboat. But don't let this nod to an early mode of transportation fool you. The Bahrain World Trade Center is as futuristic as it gets. It has electricity-generating wind turbines mounted on bridges between the center's two towers. It also features ground-level reflection pools that cool the building through evaporation.

Vancouver Convention Centre

♥ Vancouver, British Columbia

Located right on the city's waterfront, the Vancouver Convention Centre looks over the harbor to the Coast Mountains. Vancouver's marine and *terrestrial* ecosystems are important to the province's biodiversity, and the designers of the Vancouver Convention Centre believe they have a responsibility to protect them. A "skirt" around the portion of the center that was built on piles over the water forms a complete shoreline ecosystem. The centre is home to the largest living roof in Canada. At 6 acres (2.4 hectares), the roof features more than 400,000 native plants and grasses. The roof is also an insulator. This means it can help heat and cool the building. Some 240,000 bees in four colonies on the roof help pollinate plants and provide honey. The center also prioritizes eco-friendly materials, including wood from sustainably managed forests in British Columbia.

The Bahrain World Trade Center is the first commercial building to fully integrate three large-scale wind turbines into its design.

BUENA VISTA IMAGES/GETTY IMAGES

Green roofs, like this one at the Vancouver Convention Centre, are covered in soil and vegetation. They play an important role in supporting biodiversity in urban areas.

MAX LINDENTHALER/SHUTTERSTOCK.COM

Jessica Rose

JUNKITECTURE

Here's a word you might not be familiar with—*junkitecture*. This tongue twister means exactly what it sounds like. It's a combination of *junk* and *architecture*. Junkitecture uses materials that would otherwise be sent to a landfill to build useful structures. For example:

Artist Christopher Fennell used scraps from yellow school buses to create a bus-stop shelter in Athens, Georgia.

Recycloop is an outdoor pavilion in the Netherlands made from kitchen sinks.

The Naurvik project in Gjoa Haven, Nunavut, uses recycled shipping containers for growing fresh, affordable food year-round. This is especially important in Nunavut's cold climate. *Naurvik* means "growing place" in Inuinnaqtun.

Junkitecture can result in textures and shapes that you might not expect to see in a building. In this example, colorful glass bottles were incorporated into a structure's design.
IRINA274/GETTY IMAGES

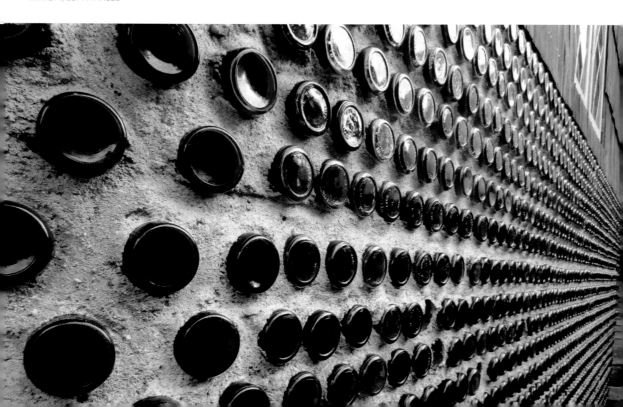

BIRD-FRIENDLY BUILDING DESIGN

In Canada, 16 to 42 million birds die each year because they collide with windows. The number is much higher in the United States, where 365 to 988 million of our feathered friends die from collisions each year. You might be wondering why birds don't simply fly *around* buildings to avoid collisions. There are many reasons birds collide with windows. Birds can become disoriented by artificial light, for example. They can also get confused by reflections of trees or sky they see in windows, thinking they see habitat or an open pathway. Even dark windows can look like tunnels to fly through.

Because they are vital to ecosystems, birds need to be conserved. They're important for controlling pests and pollinating plants, and their poop acts as fertilizer that helps land and aquatic plants grow. And, quite simply, birds are fascinating to watch and enjoy. The good news is that preventing bird collisions is possible and actually quite simple. Creative people, including architects, are designing buildings with birds in mind.

IDEAS TAKING FLIGHT

Bird-friendly building design incorporates materials and technologies that reduce threats to birds and can be beautiful to look at too.

Screens, Shutters and Sunshades: Buildings with a lot of clear or reflective glass are especially dangerous for birds. Architectural elements such as screens, shutters and sunshades on the outside of buildings provide visual cues that can stop birds from flying into windows.

Other Visual Cues: Marking glass with designs or images helps make windows more visible to birds. Patterns, murals or etchings are visual cues that let birds know they can't fly through a window or glass walkway.

Bird-Friendly Building Materials: Birds are most likely to fly into glass. They're less confused when they see concrete or metal. However, nobody likes a building with no windows! Reducing the amount of glass in a building can reduce collisions, while also saving energy on heating and cooling. Choosing stained or frosted glass helps, too. That way, some light can still get in.

Lights Out! Blinding artificial light can disorient birds. Turning off lights at night is one way to avoid collisions.

Big cities in North America, including Toronto, New York City and Ottawa, have bird-friendly design guidelines to help architects and engineers. Guidelines aren't applicable only to skyscrapers, universities and apartment buildings. You'll also see bird-friendly design in bus shelters and highway noise barriers.

You don't have to be an architect to make your home or school more bird friendly. For example, you can create a bird-friendly decal, move indoor plants away from windows, or close blinds and curtains to reduce reflections.

According to Nature Canada, there are three billion fewer birds in North America today than in 1970. Cats, collisions with buildings and loss of habitat are the major reasons for this decline.

You can create your own bird-friendly decals to help reduce bird collisions at your home or school. Do a simple internet search to find instructions.
ELVA ETIENNE/GETTY IMAGES

If you're eating at the Javits Center, chances are your meal is made using ingredients harvested from the center's green roof. The roof is also home to certain bird species, including a large herring gull colony that, in 2022, consisted of 150 nests.

FELIX LIPOV/SHUTTERSTOCK.COM

BIRD-FRIENDLY SUCCESS STORIES

The Javits Center is a convention center in New York City. For a long time it was the scene of many bird collisions. The addition of patterned glass panels changed that. Since the building was renovated, bird deaths have decreased by 90 percent.

The Javits Center also has a 6.75-acre (2.73-hectare) green roof, which is a habitat for 35 bird species, five bat species and thousands of insects. It is also home to a one-acre (0.4-hectare) farm that provides up to 40,000 pounds (18,144 kilograms) of food each year.

Here are a few other examples of bird-friendly buildings:

Toronto Metropolitan University Student Learning Centre
📍 Toronto

The Orange Cube
📍 Lyon

Los Angeles Convention Center
📍 Los Angeles

Aqua Tower
📍 Chicago

Vanessa Hum has a small business where she creates signage for events. She never thought her art could also help protect bird species.

VANESSA HUM

The Bird-Safe Campus Team at the University of Ottawa uses data dating back to 2014 to recommend bird-safe glass treatments on campus, like this one by Vanessa Hum.
VANESSA HUM

Meet a Bird-Friendly Mural Artist: VANESSA HUM

📍 Burnaby, British Columbia

Growing up, Vanessa Hum thought she had to choose between a career in art or in science. That changed when she began using her art skills to create murals that prevent birds from colliding with windows. In 2021 Hum was studying environmental science at Carleton University in Ottawa. She began volunteering with an organization called Safe Wings Ottawa. Through research, prevention and rescue, the organization works to reduce the number of birds that die from window collisions. As a volunteer, Hum patrolled the campus for birds that had died or been injured from window collisions.

"Eventually I had the opportunity to create my first bird-friendly mural at the University of Ottawa with the help of volunteers from Safe Wings," says Hum. "This opportunity has combined my passion for art, my degree in environmental science and my love for birds." The project was especially important because the University of Ottawa is located near the Ottawa River, which attracts many bird species during their migration.

Hum's bird-friendly mural appears on a glass walkway connecting two University of Ottawa buildings. It was created over four days using oil-based paint markers. The mural reduces the transparency of the glass walkway. This means birds don't get confused and think they can fly right through the glass. Since completing that first mural, Hum has created others, including at a branch of the Ottawa Public Library.

"I love showing people my murals and then educating them on their true purpose," says Hum, who went on to attend Simon Fraser University in Burnaby, British Columbia, to earn a master's degree in biology, studying bird collisions. "I can't believe that a year ago I wasn't even aware of the solutions to bird and window collisions. Now I'm in BC researching them!" she says.

"It is very special to have passion for both art and science!
They are different, but they can connect."

—Vanessa Hum

61

Wildlife bridges are sometimes called *ecoducts*. This is an aerial view of one in Dwingelderveld National Park in the Netherlands.

RUDMER ZWERVER/SHUTTERSTOCK.COM

Dusky leaf monkeys, or dusky langurs, are mostly found in Malaysia, Myanmar and Thailand.

ALBERT WRIGHT/GETTY IMAGES

CREATIVE CORRIDORS

Birds and other pollinators aren't the only creatures that sometimes require help staying safe in our world. Car collisions kill more than one million animals *every day*. The use of wildlife corridors is a creative way to reduce habitat fragmentation and fatalities. Combining building, landscape and garden design, wildlife corridors are bridges or tunnels that provide animals with a safe place to cross over or under highways and other busy roads.

Jo Leen Yap, a wildlife researcher in Malaysia, started a project to save dusky langurs, also known as dusky leaf monkeys. She created an aerial bridge made from recycled fire hoses to help the primates cross a busy road in Penang National Park.

The Burnham Wildlife Corridor in Chicago is another example of a creative corridor. This essential migration route includes plants that are native to the area and feed wildlife, including birds, caterpillars and butterflies. It also includes innovative public art that encourages people to pause and reflect on the natural world around them, such as *Sankofa for the Earth* by artists Arlene Turner-Crawford and Dorian Sylvain. The piece, which features a brightly colored mythical sankofa bird, is made from recycled materials and repurposed wood.

FASHION-FORWARD DESIGN

You've read about the design of buildings and other structures, and how it can positively and negatively affect the environment. There's another type of design worth examining—fashion design.

Fashion is a form of creative expression that can say a lot about you, your personality and what you value. When you're shopping for new clothes, you probably think about what colors, fabrics and styles you prefer. But have you ever stopped to think about the environmental impact of the clothes you wear? Here are a few staggering statistics:

It takes 2,000 gallons (7,500 liters) of water to make one pair of jeans.

Approximately 20 percent of wastewater worldwide comes from fabric dyeing and treatment.

The fashion industry is responsible for about 10 percent of annual global carbon emissions.

Canadians purchase 70 new articles of clothing, on average, each year.

Donating clothes is a great way to clear your closet. However, thrift stores sometimes receive too many items to resell, and those things often end up in landfills. That's why reducing the amount of clothing we buy is important.
SUNDRY PHOTOGRAPHY/SHUTTERSTOCK.COM

FAST FASHION

Fast fashion is the mass production of trendy, cheaply made clothing. The clothes are usually made from unsustainable materials that are not meant to last long and are shipped from far away, contributing to greenhouse gas emissions. Fast fashion sometimes relies on child labor to produce clothing inexpensively. According to UNICEF, 160 million children around the world are engaged in labor in various industries. Child labor is defined by the International Labor Organization as work that deprives children of their childhood, potential and dignity. Child labor is harmful to their physical and mental development.

THE FASHION INDUSTRY STEPS UP

More than ever, consumers are choosing to wear clothes that are made ethically and sustainably—and fashion brands are listening. Some companies are participating in the circular fashion movement. Circular fashion is part of the circular economy. It calls for recycling, upcycling, reclaiming, repairing and thrifting.

Anne Mulaire is a Canadian fashion brand. It was founded by Andréanne Mulaire Dandeneau, whose fashion designs embrace her Anishinaabe and French Métis heritage. The brand uses natural fabrics made without the use of pesticides, herbicides or chemical fertilizers, to reduce damage to the planet. Clothing fabric is hand cut so that none goes to waste. Anne Mulaire also offers alterations and repair to extend the life of clothing.

Sustainable fashion brands are also using creative reuse in amazing ways. You don't have to look further than the sneaker industry for examples. Undo For Tomorrow, which began in Rio de Janeiro and is now based in Lisbon, is an animal-friendly shoe brand that uses natural and recycled materials. The company even uses discarded party balloons and leftover tires to make lightweight rubber soles.

WHAT CAN YOU DO?

Let's face it—buying luxury clothing can be expensive. The good news is that you can make sustainable fashion choices without having to buy designer clothing. You just have to get creative.

Mend your own clothing. Sometimes we throw away clothing simply because a zipper doesn't work or there's a hole in the knee of a pair of pants. Through simple sewing techniques, you can repair a seam, darn a sock or even cover a stain. This is called *visible mending*.

Shop secondhand or vintage. You never know what you'll find when you go thrifting.

Host a clothing swap. Just like an art-supply swap, a clothing swap is a fun activity that keeps items out of the landfill.

Use fabric scraps. If your clothing is beyond repair, use the scraps to make a scrunchie, use them as rags or incorporate them into an art project.

Eskilstuna, a city in Sweden, is the home of ReTuna Återbruksgalleria, the world's first recycling mall. The shopping center sells only items that have been recycled, reused or sustainably produced. It's located beside the city's recycling center. Visitors can drop off reusable toys, furniture, clothes and other items, which are then redistributed to stores in the mall.

©LINA ÖSTLING, RETUNA

FIVE
ARTIVISM AND CRAFTIVISM

ART IS A POWERFUL TOOL that people of all ages can use to express their concerns about the environment and other important social issues. Young people especially are using art as a way to have their voices heard and to inspire change.

WHAT IS ARTIVISM?

The word *artivism* is the combination of the words *art* and **activism**. Artivism combines the power of creativity with a specific and strategic goal. It can be used to **protest** something that the creator or creators think is unfair or unjust. It is peaceful and persuasive, and it forces people to pay attention. Artivism comes in many forms, from eye-catching signage at protests or rallies to songs, poems, dance, drama and digital media.

A young activist in Hamilton, ON, uses art to convey a message at a protest.
JESSICA ROSE

67

YOUR MESSAGE MATTERS!

Artivism is accessible. This means anyone can be an artivist—including you! You don't have to be a professional artist (or even a very skilled artist) to be an artivist. All you need are some art supplies, some creativity and something to say. Artivism can be done, and led, by ordinary people who want to create meaningful change. Many artivists use DIY methods of artmaking that don't require a lot of resources, including money, to make. Zines and posters are simple and effective ways to communicate a message.

CALLING ALL CLIMATE ARTIVISTS

Around the world, millions of people in hundreds of cities have participated in climate crisis protests. They are often young people worried about their futures on a warming planet. Their posters include catchy slogans such as *There Is No Planet B* and *Don't Be a Fool! Keep the Earth Cool*. The posters are written in many different languages. Some posters don't need words at all. A simple drawing of a sad Earth can convey a moving message. That's artivism!

Many climate crisis protests are part of the Global Climate Strike movement, which was started by Greta Thunberg in 2018. The youth-led Fridays for Future movement encourages young people to get involved by attending protests, signing petitions or joining campaigns that work to reduce global warming. The movement's purpose is to put pressure on people who make laws, encouraging them to take action.

ART WORKS!

As you've read, visual art is often used to raise awareness about the climate crisis. Other artists use different art forms to bring attention to the problem. Here are just a few examples.

Cherie Dimaline is an author, editor and member of the Métis Nation of Ontario. Her book *The Marrow Thieves* and its sequel, *Hunting by Stars*, look at a future wrecked by the climate crisis.

Xiuhtezcatl Roske-Martinez is an American rapper and activist. Also known as X, he uses his music and lyrics to inspire people to take environmental issues seriously.

Davalois Fearon is a choreographer and dancer who is the artistic director of Davalois Fearon Dance. Educating others through dance is an important part of her work and includes being vocal about water scarcity and global water issues affected by climate change.

WHAT CAN YOU DO?

There doesn't need to be a protest planned in your community for you to get active! You can create a poster to display in a window or show to your classmates. Or design a flyer to distribute to friends. Your poster or flyer doesn't have to focus only on an issue. It could provide information about an event too, such as a community cleanup or a bioblitz in your area.

Here are a few tips to get you started:

Sometimes people who think pollinator gardens look messy don't realize that a variety of flowers can be beneficial to pollinators.
SIMON COLLINS/DREAMSTIME.COM

Ask yourself which **medium** you will use to convey your message. You could create a digital poster on your computer or phone, or use printed materials instead.

Come up with a catchy slogan or simple message, or use a powerful image instead. Or do both!

If you're designing a print poster, think about the supplies you will use. Don't forget about the sustainable art supplies you read about in chapter 1.

Figure out how you will display or distribute your work of art so it gets seen.

Stream of Dreams is an example of a community art project with many contributors. It's been operating for over 20 years.

BAY AREA RESTORATION COUNCIL

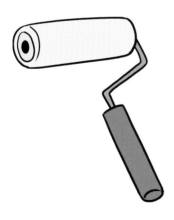

LET'S LOOK AT ART

There are many examples of artivism around us. You might see a mural in a public park or hear a song on the radio that has a goal of inspiring change. Here are a few examples,

Teaching Walls

📍 Tannis Nielsen, Toronto, Ontario

Tannis Nielsen is a multidisciplinary artist of Métis, Anishinaabe and Danish ancestry, who has used large murals to spark important conversations about Indigenous access to land and water. *Gchi-twaawendan NIbi/Honour the Water* is a tribute to water activist Josephine Mandamin. She walked more than 10,500 miles (17,000 kilometers) around the Great Lakes to raise awareness of the importance of protecting water from pollution. *N'gekaajig Kidowog/ My Elders Said* is 28 portraits of local teachers and elders. The combined length of Nielson's murals is 420 feet (128 meters). That's longer than a football field! Located in downtown Toronto, Nielsen's murals were created in collaboration with local Indigenous youth. "I think it is important for established artists to mentor the next

generation as a way of giving back to the community and passing on teachings to them," she said in an interview with the Art Gallery of Ontario.

Stream of Dreams
📍 Canada-Wide

Stream of Dreams is an eco-education program that teaches students and their communities about their local watersheds, streams, rivers and oceans. It encourages young people to make positive changes that conserve and protect water. The program also raises awareness about water conservation through a community mural project. Stream of Dreams started in 2000 after someone dumped toxic material into a storm drain in the Byrne Creek Watershed, located in Burnaby, British Columbia. The toxin killed all the aquatic life in Byrne Creek, including 5,000 fish. Today you'll find Stream of Dreams fish murals in many cities across Canada. Each student and staff member at schools participating in the program paints and contributes a colorful fish to the mural. You might spot them "swimming" along fences in your own neighborhood.

The mission of the Children's Museum of Art and Social Justice in Chicago is to offer a space for the voices of students. One exhibit, called *Food for Thought*, featured student artwork about the role food and food waste plays in their lives.

Just Add Water

📍 Chicago, Illinois

Just Add Water was an exhibition hosted by the Children's Museum of Art and Social Justice in Chicago. The exhibition featured a series of installations made by artists between the ages of 5 and 13. The work in this exhibition explored water as something people consume, a place people gather beside and a human right. In one installation, young artists were asked to examine their own water usage. They also used papier-mâché to illustrate the number of gallons of water used per person per day in the United States.

Turtle Crossing

📍 Hamilton, Ontario

Turtle Crossing is a program for students in Hamilton, Ontario, presented by the Bay Area Restoration Council. The program looks at the importance of the area's wetlands, which are diverse ecosystems with a variety of plants and wildlife, including turtles. Students learn about threats to local turtles, including habitat loss, predators and collisions with cars, then make their own clay turtles to use as a visual when talking to others about how human activity threatens turtles.

The Bay Area Restoration Council in Hamilton, ON, le
collective action to revitalize Hamilton Harbour. Turt
Crossing is one of the council's education programs.
BAY AREA RESTORATION COUNCIL

ECO-ANXIETY AND ART

Climate change and other environmental issues cause anxiety in people of all ages. The fear of ecological disaster, and worry about the future of the planet, is called *eco-anxiety*. Some artists find that creating art is a positive way to deal with stress. That's because art gives us a chance to use our imaginations to process difficult feelings. We can also use art to reimagine what we want the future to look like.

In 2022 Gallery 1C03 at the University of Winnipeg hosted an exhibit called *Worried Earth: Eco-Anxiety and Entangled Grief*. It explored how worry about climate change affects day-to-day life. Many of the seven artists in the show used sustainable materials. For example, Kuh Del Rosario's art included cement, plaster, pulped paper, dried orange peels and various types of seeds. Her sculptures often have many lives. She takes them apart and repurposes them for new works of art.

Crafting may have a positive effect on mental health. It can trigger the release of dopamine, a brain chemical that influences how you feel. One study of 3,500 knitters found that 81 percent of knitters with depression said knitting made them feel happier.

Monica Figueroa (middle) worries about her family in Colombia, who are experiencing the impact of climate change firsthand. Drought and unpredictable rainy seasons make it difficult for farmers to earn a living. Here Monica is pictured with other members of Edmonton Youth for Climate. EMILY BONNANI, COURTESY OF MONICA FIGUEROA

Meet an Artivist: MONICA FIGUEROA

📍 Edmonton, Alberta

Edmonton's Monica Figueroa is using art to navigate eco-anxiety and express her concerns about the environment. After moving to Canada in 2019, Figueroa was shocked by the country's reliance on fossil fuel to heat and cool homes, power vehicles and transport goods all over the world. She joined Edmonton Youth for Climate, an organization that educates, engages and empowers people to take action on the climate crisis.

The group hosted an in-person art build where participants could share food, ideas and stories while creating art. The event was part of Visions for the Future: The Edmonton Climate Art Project.

"Climate change is often posed as a problem for scientists only to understand and solve," says Figueroa. "But in reality, it is a human problem. And one of the most human forms of expression is art."

At the art build, artists created paintings, poems, letters, memes, songs, collages and drawings. Pieces reflected many emotions,

including anger, fear, despair, hope, love and resilience. "Young people often feel very anxious about climate change," says Figueroa. "Our starting point in the environmental movement is not one of trying to convince people about facts and figures, but trying to convince people that they should be angry, fearful and concerned too."

Figueroa is studying physics and hopes to continue her education in oceanographic and atmospheric science. She has also interned at the Max Planck Institute for Meteorology in Germany to study the effects of cloud formation on climate change. She is living proof that art and science don't have to be separate. Both can work together to create a better future.

"We often feel things in our hearts before we know it in our heads. This, I think, is especially true for youth," says Figueroa. "Creative spaces might be a more effective space to deal with climate anxiety than a lecture hall."

FEELING CRAFTY?

Similar to artivism, craftivism is using creativity as a form of protest or to advance social causes. The goal of craftivism is political or social change. It involves craft skills such as sewing, knitting, weaving, embroidery or woodworking. Craftivism is often called a gentle or slow form of activism. Craftivists might work alone, or they might craft as part of a collective. (A collective is a group of people with a common interest or goal.) Throughout history, crafting has been overlooked as a form of art. Some people think that's because, traditionally, crafting has been done by women. Today it can be seen as a powerful way to create change.

This example of craftivism was part of the Craftivist Collective's Dream-Making project, where people hand-stitched their hopes and dreams onto a cloud to manifest a positive change they wished to see in the world.

SARAH P CORBETT/CRAFTIVIST COLLECTIVE

Yarn bombing is an example of temporary art. It's not meant to last forever, but that doesn't mean it can't have a huge impact!

ELENA DIJOUR/SHUTTERSTOCK.COM

Stitches for Survival was a project made up of more than 1,000 knitted, crocheted or sewn fabric panels, each containing a climate message, from crafters across the United Kingdom. They were stitched together to create a scarf 1.5-miles (2.4-kilometers) long for display during the COP26 Climate Conference in November 2021. After this event, some of the panels were repurposed and made into blankets and mats. They were distributed to refugees and homeless people who needed them.

A CLOSE-KNIT COMMUNITY

A knit-in is a form of craftivism where knitters gather in a public space to knit and draw attention to an important issue. Sometimes crafters don't even have to gather in person. The Climate Coalition, the largest group of people dedicated to action against the climate crisis in the United Kingdom, encouraged people everywhere to knit a green heart to raise awareness about climate change issues. The social media campaign encouraged crafters to share their creations using the hashtag #ShowTheLove. The green heart symbolized love and encouraged people to think about things they care about and what might be lost because of the climate crisis.

Another popular form of craftivism is yarn bombing. It's a form of street art or public art that can draw attention to important issues and reclaim underused or abandoned spaces. Nina Elliott is a textile artist and yarn bomber in Newfoundland. During the COVID-19 pandemic, she covered 1.2 miles (2 kilometers) of a street in her town of Twillingate with colorful yarn art. It encouraged people to go outside and explore their environment during lockdown, when galleries were closed. Elliott hopes her art brings joy to people who are feeling stressed or anxious. Her goal is to create a happier and healthier community through public art.

Before you start yarn bombing your neighborhood, think about its environmental impact. While yarn bombing can be fun, some people think it's wasteful. That's because the yarn is often removed from city parks and other property, ending up in the trash. Instead of creating a temporary yarn installation, create something permanent that you can display at home or in a public place with permission.

RAISE YOUR VOICE!

I hope that reading this book has inspired you to create art that puts the environment first. The ways you express yourself can build a more sustainable world! You have a right to a safe and healthy environment. You also have a right to have your voice heard. Instead of simply making art because it's fun, you can make art because it's purposeful and revolutionary!

While writing this book, I was lucky enough to talk to passionate artists and organizers who are already making Earth a better place to live. And while their work is important, I was struck by how possible it is for us *all* to create change through art. You don't need expensive supplies or the biggest canvas to be an artist with an impact. You can start in small, meaningful ways by being mindful of your artistic practices and what your art is trying to say.

GET ORGANIZED!

So let's make art! Start by asking yourself what environmental issues are most important to you. Through your art you can elevate countless causes, such as biodiversity loss, traffic congestion and habitat fragmentation. Think about *why* and *how* you will use art to make a difference.

You can also tell others about some of the amazing artists and work you've read about in this book. Elevating their work and causes is an important part of communicating their message. And, finally, get out of your comfort zone. One of the best things about artmaking is it doesn't have to be perfect. Try a variety of materials and new techniques and use unfamiliar mediums. You never know what you'll create and who you might inspire!

Making art can convey your own message, but that's not all it can do. Your creativity can also boost your confidence and help you relax.

DUSAN STANKOVIC/GETTY IMAGES

ART WORKS!

One simple way to be part of an environmental movement is to participate in an advocacy day, week or month. You'll be joining people from around the world, uniting for a cause. Here are a few examples to get you started:

International Day for Biological Diversity: Also known as Biodiversity Day, this day happens every May and looks at the important role biodiversity plays in our daily life. Biodiversity is essential to healthy ecosystems, waterways and the food we grow and eat.

Waste Reduction Week in Canada: This important week takes place every October. Is there a better time to try out some of the creative-reuse projects you've read about in this book?

Plastic Free July: We can all be part of a plastic-pollution solution. Plastic Free July is a global movement that helps millions of people do their part to reduce plastic waste. The movement has inspired more than 100 million participants in 190 countries around the world. This July take a pledge to avoid single-use plastics for a month—or longer.

Express Yourself: Let's be honest. If you're like some people, showing your art to the world might be intimidating. But it doesn't have to be. Even if you show it to one person, you're telling them about an issue they might not be aware of, and that's enough!

GLOSSARY

accessibility—the quality or characteristic of something that makes an approach, entry or use possible

activism—the practice of taking action to achieve political or social goals

artificial intelligence (AI)—the capability of a machine to imitate human behavior

big-box store—a store that occupies a large physical space, offers a wide variety of products and is part of a larger chain of stores

biodiversity—the variety of living things in a specific place

biomimicry—learning from and imitating nature in engineering or invention to find creative solutions to everyday problems

carbon-neutral—having a balance between emitting carbon dioxide and absorbing it from the atmosphere

creativity—the ability to use one's imagination to produce something that is original

curator—a person who cares for and develops a collection of art

deforestation—the clearing, or cutting down, of forests

diverting—turning from one course or direction to another

durability—ability to withstand wear, pressure or damage

ecological design—an approach to designing goods and services that considers their environmental impact and life cycle

environmentalism—a movement concerned about protecting the environment

erosion—the process of slowly wearing away or impairing

fine art—art made with the purpose of being beautiful, not functional

habitat fragmentation—a process in which human activity or natural disaster divides large habitats into smaller, unconnected habitats, making migrating or finding food difficult for wildlife

ingenuity—the quality of being clever, original and inventive

invasive species—plants and animals that are not originally from a specific area and can cause harm to their new environment

land disturbance—a change in soil, land or vegetation, often the result of human activities

landfills—large portions of land where waste material is disposed of by burying it and covering it with soil

leatherwork—articles made of leather

medium—the material or method used for artistic expression, such as paint on canvas (the plural form of the word is *media*)

microbes—living things that are too small to be seen by the human eye

microplastics—extremely small pieces of plastic, less than five millimeters in size

permafrost—subsurface layer of soil that remains frozen all year

polymer—a very large molecule made of many tiny molecules layered together in a repeating pattern

protest—express (or an expression of) disapproval or objection to something, often in the form of a large gathering

purchasing power—the ability to purchase goods and services

raw materials—materials that have not been processed and can be used to produce other items

renewable energy—energy from a resource that can be replaced naturally, such as wind and solar power. Unlike fossil fuels, renewable-energy sources don't run out.

respiration—a process in which organisms use oxygen to break down food molecules to get the chemical energy they need for cell functions

revitalizes—gives new life to

surplus—the amount left over after a need or use has been satisfied

sustainable—able to be maintained over time, used in reference to harvesting or using resources in a way that ensures there will be enough for future generations

synthetic—made from artificial substances, often to imitate a natural product

terrestrial—of the earth; living on or growing from land

unorthodox—unusual or nontraditional

urban—relating to a city

waste stream—the flow and life cycle of the waste we produce

RESOURCES

PRINT

Cavalier, Darlene, Caren Cooper and Catherine Hoffman. *The Field Guide to Citizen Science: How You Can Contribute to Scientific Research and Make a Difference.* Workman Publishing Company, 2020.

Clendenan, Megan. *Fresh Air, Clean Water: Our Right to a Healthy Environment.* Orca Book Publishers, 2022.

Corbett, Sarah. *How to Be a Craftivist: The Art of Gentle Protest.* Unbound, 2017.

Curtis, Andrea. *City Streets Are for People.* Groundwood Books, 2022.

Delisle, Raina. *Fashion Forward: Striving for Sustainable Style.* Orca Book Publishers, 2022.

Eierman, Kim. *The Pollinator Victory Garden: Win the War on Pollinator Decline with Ecological Gardening.* Quarry Books, 2020

Fulop, Lily. *Wear, Repair, Repurpose: A Maker's Guide to Mending and Upcycling Clothes.* Countryman Press, 2020.

Guy, Cylita. *Chasing Bats and Tracking Rats: Urban Ecology, Community Science, and How We Share Our Cities.* Annick Press, 2021.

Kaner, Etta. *Earth-Friendly Buildings, Bridges and More: The Eco-Journal of Corry Lapont.* Kids Can Press, 2012.

Thomas, Isabel. *This Book Is Not Garbage: 50 Ways to Ditch Plastic, Reduce Trash and Save the World!* Random House Children's Books, 2018.

ONLINE

Art & Object: artandobject.com/articles/artivism-making-difference-through-art

Bird-Safe Design and Standards: birdsafe.ca/design-standards

Citizen Science Projects: science.nasa.gov/citizenscience

Creative City Network of Canada, Public Art Resources: creativecity.ca/programs/publicart

Fatal Light Awareness Program (FLAP) Canada: flap.org

Hamilton Pollinator Paradise Project: hamiltonpollinatorparadise.org

Nature Canada: naturecanada.ca

Pollinator Pathmaker: pollinator.art/pathmaker

ACKNOWLEDGMENTS

This book was born out of a deep appreciation for the artists and environmentalists who work tirelessly to create a more sustainable present and future. Thank you especially to everyone who shared their work and stories in this book. I would like to thank the team at Orca Book Publishers, especially Kirstie Hudson, for believing in a book about the value and impact of art. This book would not be possible without the encouragement of many members of Hamilton's vibrant literary scene. Thank you also to Hamilton's Biodiversity Action Plan working group for the constant inspiration and the work you do to protect and enhance our city. Thank you to my family—Jim, Shelly and Jenni—and to the many teachers who encouraged my love of reading, writing and exploring. They include Martyn Olenick, Helmut Manzl and my late first-grade teacher, Wendy Ernst, who, 30 years ago, I promised that I'd thank in my first book. And, most important, thanks to every young person—I know you can change the world with your art.

ALISTAIR BERG/GETTY IMAGES

INDEX

*Page numbers in **bold** indicate an image caption.*

ORCA Think

THE MORE YOU KNOW...

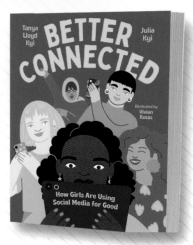

BETTER CONNECTED
Tanya Lloyd Kyi
Julia Kyi
Illustrated by Vivian Rosas
How Girls Are Using Social Media for Good

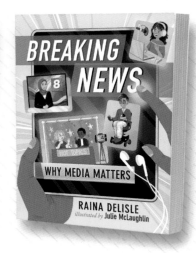

BREAKING NEWS
WHY MEDIA MATTERS
RAINA DELISLE
illustrated by Julie McLaughlin

FINDING HOME
Jen Sookfong Lee
The Journey of Immigrants and Refugees
ILLUSTRATED BY Drew Shannon

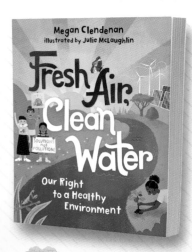

Fresh Air, Clean Water
Megan Clendenan
illustrated by Julie McLaughlin
Our Right to a Healthy Environment

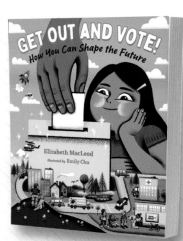

GET OUT AND VOTE!
How You Can Shape the Future
Elizabeth MacLeod
illustrated by Emily Chu

GOOD FOOD, BAD WASTE
Let's Eat for the Planet
Erin Silver
illustrated by Suharu Ogawa

RIGHT TO LIVE

RiGHT to SPeak UP!

EQUALITY = FOR = ALL

Right to Live Free of Discrimination

RIGHT TO LEARN

freedom to Think

THE MORE YOU GROW

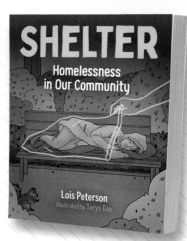

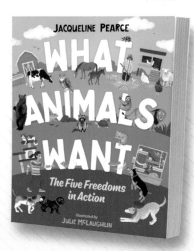

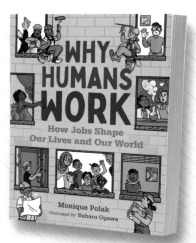

WHAT'S THE BIG IDEA?

The **Orca Think** series introduces us to the issues making headlines in the world today. It encourages us to question, connect and take action for a better future. With those tools we can all become better citizens. Now that's smart thinking!

JESSICA ROSE is a writer, editor and arts organizer who lives and works in Hamilton, Ontario. A passionate advocate for people and places, she works for a number of not-for-profit organizations focused on literacy, the arts, the environment, health and food security. A graduate of Carleton University's School of Journalism, her writing includes the essay "Reclaiming Hamilton Through Artistic and Environmental Interventions" in *Reclaiming Hamilton: Essays from the New Ambitious City* (Wolsak and Wynn), *Creating Healthy Communities* (Rubicon Publishing) and the City of Hamilton Biodiversity Action Plan (BAP).

JARETT SITTER is a mixed-media illustrator and animator of Chinese, German and Polish descent. He graduated with a BFA in new media from the University of Lethbridge and now works full-time as a freelance artist. In 2022 his children's book *The Curious Invitation: Braving the Unknown*, created for William Joseph Agency, won three Anvil Awards. Jarett lives in Calgary.